Old BEARSDEN

by

William M. McKinlay and Ian B. Hamilton

Schaw Convalescent Home is one of the landmarks of the district. Built in 1895 by Miss Marjory Shanks Schaw, in memory of her brother, the building was gifted to Glasgow Royal Infirmary. It was requisitioned as a troop hospital during the First World War and in 1986 it became the Schaw Auxiliary Hospital with room only for 75 patients. It has since become the Lynedoch Private Nursing Home.

© William M. McKinlay and Ian B. Hamilton, 1997
First Published in the United Kingdom, 1997
By Stenlake Publishing
Telephone/fax: 01290 551122

ISBN 1 84033 011 2

Schaw Home overlooking a row of houses on Drymen Road. These were called 'The Beeches' and the Courthill houses are on the left. The area in the foreground is now taken up by Stirling Drive but this development has not interfered with the Manse Burn which still runs through The Beeches' back gardens.

Foreword

In bringing together this selection of postcards we have tried to 'look backward' on Bearsden and show some buildings which are no longer there. The book also features areas, such as Bearsden Cross and Canniesburn Toll, that have changed extensively over the years. Of particular interest are the rooms of Drewsteignton Home School, which will be seen by many readers for the first time.

Many of the postcards were written by maids in the large houses to other maids across the city and some of the messages show just how fast the mail service was in the early 1900s - one classic message says, 'Will see you tonight at 8.00 o'clock.'

Some of the views in this book are today hidden by the planting of forest trees in small gardens. These trees look nice when they are young, but once established they 'reach for the sky' and will no doubt outlive most of us. It is interesting to note that some postcards can be dated by the size of the trees!

We hope our efforts are of interest not only to the older residents who may remember some of what has changed but also to the young, perhaps moving into Bearsden for the first time.

William M. McKinlay and Ian B. Hamilton, Bearsden, 1997.

Bearsden viewed from Schaw Home, *c*1925. In the centre of the picture is the Home's lodge house where the gardener lived. The plot where he grew flowers and vegetables for the home is just out of the picture to the left. The lodge is now a 24 Hour Care Centre for the elderly and housebound, and the houses of Schaw Court and Kirk Care now stand on the lawn.

The foundation stone for the New Kilpatrick Parish Church Halls, right, (now referred to as the 'Old Halls') was laid in September 1934. The building was paid for by the congregation and opened in April of the following year.

New Kilpatrick Manse, Bearsden

The manse of New Kilpatrick Parish Church was built in 1837. Two of the windows in the upper story, facing the glebe, had been blocked off, possibly to prevent payment of the Window Tax which was repealed in 1851. From 1875 it was the childhood home of the artist Jessie M. King, member of the famous 'Glasgow Girls' group. The manse was replaced by a new one on the same site in 1965 but the area is now overgrown and the glebe has become a large car park.

AERIAL VIEW. BEARSDEN

A84897

An aerial view, c1924, showing Bearsden Cross and beyond. Drymen Road runs from bottom left to top right.

Drymen Road looking south towards Bearsden Cross. The elegant silver birches by the entrance to the Public Halls (just out of picture to the right) were unfortunately cut down in the late 1960s when the area around the hall was turned into another car park.

Courthill, Drymen Road, Bearsden

These houses at Courthill on Drymen Road were at one time the most northerly in Bearsden and were built around 1870. To the right is the start of one of the many right-of-ways in the district, most of which led to the Parish Church. This particular one gives a good short cut to Stockiemuir Road.

NEWKIRK, BEARSDEN.

The view northwards through Bearsden Cross, c1908. The houses and shops of New Kirk were built in 1906. At the far right of the block in the centre is Gillies newsagent for whom this card was printed. The short-lived 'New School' on the right was built in 1880 only to be demolished in 1910.

The junction of New Kirk Square and Roman Road, *c*1910. At this time the Post Office was at the first doorway on Roman Road, immediately before the striped blind.

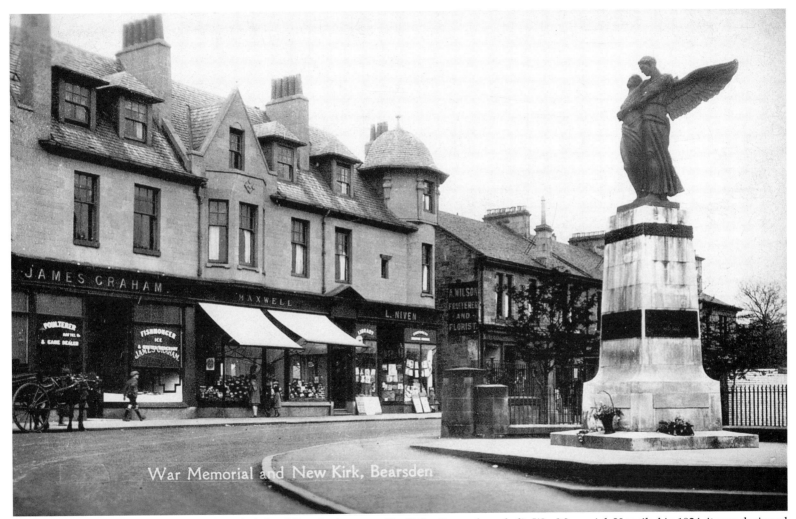

War Memorial and New Kirk, Bearsden

New Kirk Square with Douglas Place directly behind Bearden's unusually distinctive and symbolic War Memorial. Unveiled in 1924, it was designed by Alexander Proudfoot R.S.A. and the winged figure represents the national consciousness of the sacrifice made by the country's youth, symbolised by the stricken figure in its arms.

Douglas Place, c1900. The building was erected in 1880 and to make way for it a row of small cottages had to be demolished and a large tree cut down. Local children counted the rings and agreed that the tree must have been over 100 years old. The Post Office now occupies the Cycle Shop and part of the Italian Warehouseman next door, which later became the grocers' branch of Milngavie Co-op. Thorn Road with Meldrum's Tree and the North Church is in the background.

Old Coaching House, Bearsden. 1207.

The Old Coaching Inn, next to Meldrum's stables, was opposite the main entrance to the North Church. It was a favourite meeting place for both villagers and the lairds of the neighbourhood, and was probably the first licensed premises in the district. There is a story that one evening when entertaining some cronies, the old Laird of Garscadden died in his chair. Someone noticed but did not consider it important enough to interrupt the conversation! Both the inn and the stables were demolished in 1906 to make way for New Kirk Square.

A quiet residential area at the junction of Thorn Drive and Iain Road. These houses were built during the late 1920s but since then further developments have taken place. Courthill, in the centre background, has been taken up by housing and on the north side of the hill there is an artificial ski slope. To the left, on Hungry Hill, there now stands the students' quarters of St Andrew's College and behind these another residential development, St Andrew's Rise.

Drewsteignton Home School, Bearsden, Dumbartonshire

Drewsteignton Home School was opened in 1922 by Mrs Spencer Ponsford as the only private school in the district. The first site was in Collylinn Road but after two years the school moved to this custom built building in Upper Glenburn Road. At first the school had accommodation for twenty boarders and sixty day pupils but this was later increased to 260 children at the primary stage. A second department at Ledcameroch House later increased the roll to 600 pupils. The school has now merged with The High School of Glasgow.

A Classroom
Drewsteignton Home School Bearsden Dumbartonshire.

A typical classroom in the school.

Transition Class
Drewsteignton Home School
Bearsden, Dumbartonshire.

The Transition Class was for the five year olds about to move up a year. As the presence of the rocking horse makes plain, play was important to the young boarders who were separated from their parents for the whole term.

The 'Babies' Dormitory for the youngest pupils.

U.F. Church and Manse, Bearsden

Bearsden South Church was built in 1874 'by a few friends who felt the need for a church where dissenters could worship according to their principles'. First known as New Kilpatrick United Presbyterian Church, it only became the 'South Church' in 1929. It was burned down during an air raid in March 1941 and a new church was opened on the site in 1955.

The houses and shops of Stewart Terrace, now part of Drymen Road, at the turn of the century. The Terrace was built around 1880 and was the first tenement in the village. Gabriel Hamilton's premises were later owned by H.J. Strachan the baker and are now R.S. McColl's. 'Brookwood' - now Bearsden Library - is at the end of the road with Schaw Home overlooking in the background.

Looking north on what is now Drymen Road - Stewart Terrace is the nearest block on the right. Further down the street on the right across Kirk Road is Chartwell Terrace and opposite that is the Episcopal Church, opened in 1897.

OLD SCHOOL AND ROMAN ROAD, BEARSDEN.

Looking east from Bearsden Cross along Roman Road - Meldrum's Tree is on the left. The Old School on the right was built in 1860 but demolished in 1888. Although this postcard dates from c1905, the picture was taken much earlier, probably by wealthy local resident Mr Fulton. He moved to Bearsden around 1880 and took many photographs of the district.

Roman Road, *c*1938. The boy with the bicycle was courting an assistant in Miss Niven's stationers across the road. We know this as this card was one of a series specially printed for Miss Niven's shop. The photograph was taken after 5pm on a weekday as the boys underneath the lamp had just finished work. Three were plumbers and the fourth a gardener.

St Peter's College, built in 1894 as a college for Roman Catholic priests, was sadly destroyed by fire in 1946 during renovations to remove dry rot. Notre Dame College of Education (now St Andrew's College) was built on the site and opened to students in 1968.

The library and reading room of St Peter's College. The arched window reveals the room's original purpose as the college chapel.

BEARSDEN HIGHER GRADE SCHOOL.

New Kilpatrick Public School was built in 1911, on the site of the 'New School' that was demolished in 1910. Contrary to the caption on the picture, it was for both primary and secondary pupils and was renamed Bearsden Academy in 1920. It became simply Bearsden primary after 1957 when a new Secondary School was built. This card, postmarked 1915, was sent to a young girl, a pupil of the school on holiday in Peebles, by her father. Rather cruelly he wrote, 'do you recognise the view on the other side. Love, Daddy.'

The petrol station and shops on Milngavie Road were built in the 1930s. Little has changed, but the volume of traffic has increased!

645/7 *Mains, Milngavie.*

RELIABLE SERIES

Mains House was built in 1683 and was roofed with Easdale slate which was becoming popular at the time. For many generations it was owned by the Douglas family who were heritors of New Kilpatrick Parish Church (i.e. they paid the minister and for the upkeep of the church). In 1964 this ancient house became the victim of redevelopment and was demolished to provide a site for Douglas Academy, Milngavie.

The Buchanan Retreat, Bearsden

The Buchanan Retreat was opened in 1890, the building having been paid for from legacies left by three sisters, the Misses Buchanan of Bellfield in Ayrshire. It's purpose was to provide a home for poorer members of the Buchanan clan in their elderly years. This was something of a restriction on admissions and the rules were later relaxed when it was discovered that was only accommodating fourteen men. Bearsden Burgh Council took over the building as their offices in 1962 and today, known as Boclair House, it's the offices of the recently formed East Dunbartonshire Council.

These shops at Kessington have changed little since they were built in the 1920s. Over the road, on the left, is the 1923 transformer sub-station for tramcars passing here from Glasgow via Maryhill to Milngavie. The last tramcar to Milngavie ran in 1956 and the building then became redundant. Ten years later, however, it was found a new use as Kessington Hall.

Entrance to Killermont Golf Course.
4059/4

The entrance to Glasgow Golf Club's Killermont Course - before the general use of the motor car!

The Glasgow Golf Club has a very long history, having been founded in 1787, although it has been located at Killermont since only 1904. The club house, Killermont House, is included in the list of buildings of architectural and historical interest retained by the county of Dunbartonshire. Although there has been a record of a mansion house on this site since the early 1700s, the present building dates from 1805 and is a former home of the Colquhoun family.

Killermont.

Photo by John Bogue.

This house on the ninth fairway of the Killermont course was home to the club greenkeeper. The Killermont course has a lovely woodland setting along the banks of the River Kelvin which forms part of the boundary between Bearsden and Glasgow. Killermont may be its 'home base' but Glasgow Golf Club is thought to be the only club in Britain to have a links course as well. This is the eighteen hole course at Gailes, near Irvine in Ayrshire.

Garscube Bridge from Killermont.

RELIABLE SERIES. 4040/84

Garscube Bridge over the River Kelvin by Maryhill Road. This picture was taken from the weir which controlled the water level for Garscube Mill on the right beyond the bridge.

The corn mill at Garscube was built in the early 1850s and powered by an undershot waterwheel seen to the left of the building. (The term 'undershot' describes a watermill where the water runs under the wheel, these were prevalent in flat country). The hamlet of Garscube, consisting only of some half a dozen houses was built around the mill for its workers. The mill closed in the 1930s although there were others in the district that continued to operate. The last one at Milngavie closed in 1950.

Garscube House, *c*1900. It was built in 1826 by the Colquhouns of Luss before passing into the hands of John Campbell of Succoth, Dunbartonshire. During the Second World War it was used as a nurses home and in 1948 it was announced that the house was being given to Glasgow University. However, it was demolished only seven years later.

THE BOWLING GREEN BEARSDEN.

The Bowling Green on Station Road was built in 1879. The railway separates it from the houses on Ledcameroch Crescent in the background.

Bearsden Railway Station, *c*1903. The first railway line from Glasgow Queen Street High Level Station via Cowlairs, Possilpark and Maryhill through Bearsden and Milngavie was built in 1863 as a single track and carried thirteen trains daily. The present Low Level line to Glasgow through Anniesland and tunnelling below the Forth and Clyde Canal, was completed in 1869 also as a single track. A second track was laid in 1901 and the line was electrified in 1960. The old goods yard is on the right with the houses and shops of Melville Place in the background.

The station, *c*1912. The train is *en route* to Milngavie. There were large waiting rooms on each platform and on cold days a coal fire burned brightly in the room for Glasgow passengers. At the time of this picture the station master lived in the upper story. Today it is the Beefeater Restaurant.

Melville Place and Eaton Place were two blocks of houses and shops opposite the railway station. Melville Place was built on the site of an old gas works which was run by the Partick and Maryhill Gas Co. Bearsden Post Office had its first home in Eaton Place and was combined with a grocer's shop. The message on this card reads, 'I return tomorrow by train leaving one o'clock. Expect to be in Sunderland shortly after six.' In those days the mail was as fast as the train!

St Germain's Loch as it was in the early 1900s. Today the loch is almost surrounded by houses and flats. Villagers used to skate on the loch during hard frosts but there was always a danger during the thaw and a few drownings did occur. The name of the loch dates back to before 1835 at least, as there is a record of a parish minister of the time knowing it by this name and associating it with St Germanus, a companion of St Patrick, after whom the parish is named.

CANNIESBURN TOLL, BEARSDEN

The view from Maryhill Road of the old toll house at Canniesburn where four turnpike roads met. Toll was collected here until 1883 for their upkeep. Double charges were levied on Sundays to discourage travel on the Sabbath!

Canniesburn Toll.

The toll from Switchback Road, leading on the left up Drymen Road to Bearsden Cross, and on the right to Milngavie. Just in view up the Bearsden road is the old Police Station and behind the trees in the centre of the picture was the club house of the Canniesburn Golf Club which is now a private residence. The card is postmarked 1917, well before the age of mass motor travel. Nevertheless, the figure in the centre is actually an AA patrolman.

Canniesburn Toll and New Road, Bearsden

A 1929 view of the toll when the new road was built from Anniesland but before the appearance of the present roundabout and dual carriageway.

The roundabout had been opened by the time of this 1935 picture but on the hill Canniesburn Hospital was not yet ready for use.

Canniesburn Hospital, Bearsden.

Believing that patients recovered more rapidly in an auxiliary annexe, the Royal Infirmary authorities decided to build Canniesburn Hospital on land formerly owned by Canniesburn Golf Club. The Zachary Merton Trustees agreed to co-operate by providing a wing for this purpose, but the rest of the building was reserved for paying patients 'of limited income'. The hospital was ready for use in 1938.

Lochend viewed from the hospital. Postmarked July 1944, the card was sent to an address in Staffordshire. Part of the message reads, 'the children and I were invited here when they knew about the 'flying bombs'. We were right on their route and getting them day and night.'

Canniesburn Golf Course 4th Green.

The fourth green of Canniesburn Golf Course. This nine hole course was built in 1908 on the ground later taken up by the hospital. In 1924 the Club moved to an eighteen hole course at Windyhill. This picture shows the view towards St Germain Loch before the houses of Rubislaw Drive and Lochend were built.